For the graceful and gracious Raven Wilkinson
—LS

To my Aunt Cyndy
—TT

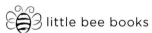 little bee books

An imprint of Bonnier Publishing USA
251 Park Avenue South, New York, NY 10010
Text copyright © 2018 by Leda Schubert
Illustrations copyright © 2018 by Theodore Taylor III
All rights reserved, including the right of reproduction in whole or in part in any form.
LITTLE BEE BOOKS is a trademark of Bonnier Publishing USA, and associated colophon
is a trademark of Bonnier Publishing USA.
Manufactured in China   HH 1017
First Edition   10 9 8 7 6 5 4 3 2 1
Library of Congress Cataloging-in-Publication Data is available upon request.

ISBN 978-1-4998-0592-5

littlebeebooks.com
bonnierpublishingusa.com

TRAILBLAZER

THE STORY OF BALLERINA RAVEN WILKINSON

BY LEDA SCHUBERT

ILLUSTRATED BY
THEODORE TAYLOR III

WITH A FOREWORD BY
MISTY COPELAND

Dear Readers,

When I was twenty-three years old, I watched a documentary called *Ballets Russes*. This was the day my life and my purpose changed. I discovered a black ballerina named Raven Wilkinson, and it was in her that I saw myself and what was possible. Raven's inspiring story is one of perseverance, dignity, hope, and strength.

The lack of diversity and representation in classical ballet is an ongoing issue. Although I was already a professional ballerina at the time I saw the film, I'm fortunate to have discovered Raven when I did. I only wish I could have known her story when I was a little girl. I'm thrilled that all young people can now be introduced to Raven through the pages of this wonderful book, *Trailblazer: The Story of Ballerina Raven Wilkinson*.

Since learning about Raven, sharing her journey and those of the many black ballerinas who have paved the way has become part of my mission. My hope is that many generations to come will be encouraged by this book and reading her story. I'm honored to call Raven my mentor and friend, and I'm so grateful that her impact and legacy are being shared.

Misty Copeland

Raven Wilkinson was born on February 2, 1935, in New York City. From the time she was a little girl, all she ever wanted to do was dance.

When Raven was only five years old, her parents took her to see the Ballet Russe de Monte Carlo. She perched on her crushed-velvet seat, heard the tympani, and cried with delight even before the curtain lifted. From that moment on, her passion for dance only grew deeper.

No black ballerina had ever danced with a major American touring troupe before. Fifteen years later, Raven Wilkinson would be the first.

On Raven's ninth birthday, her uncle gifted her with ballet lessons. Raven arrived for her first class wearing shorts and sneakers, with her knobby knees sticking out.

Her teacher, Madame Maria Swoboda, wore her red hair in a bun, loaded her fingers with rings, and smelled of strong perfume that stayed on Raven's arms after class.

"Are you French? Or maybe Spanish?" Madame asked. She didn't know what to make of the light-skinned Raven.

With Madame, Raven practiced uncountable pirouettes and pliés, arabesques and échappés. Her feet and ankles grew strong. Then she rose on her toes, dancing en pointe, defying gravity.

Madame told Raven's parents, "Raven is very talented. She will dance before kings and queens."

But for the next several years, Raven danced only for Madame.

Raven attended college at Columbia University in 1953. While a student, she auditioned twice for the Ballet Russe. A friend said to her, "They can't take you because of your race."

But Raven wouldn't give up. After her third audition, the director, Sergei Denham, said, "How would you like to be in the Ballet Russe de Monte Carlo?"

"It is my dearest dream," she said. It was now 1955 and Raven, all of twenty years old, was already a trailblazer.

The Ballet Russe traveled from the fall until the following spring every year. The troupe visited dozens of cities all over the United States, covering thousands of miles.

Each day Raven boarded the bus where everyone ate, slept, and rehearsed. "We were like a family," she said. The dancers even decorated the seats at Christmas. "Everyone wanted the back seat, where we could stretch."

They performed in simple high school auditoriums as well as fancy opera houses. Many in the audience had never seen classical dance. They shook the walls with applause and fell in love with ballet.

Shortly before Raven joined the company, the United States Supreme Court handed down a major decision in 1954. The court, in *Brown v. the Board of Education*, ordered all schools that had previously admitted only white or black students, a practice known as "segregation," to admit every student, regardless of ethnicity. For a very long time, millions of Americans had dreamed of black students and white students learning together. Across the country, many people rejoiced.

But not everyone celebrated. The Ku Klux Klan, an organization that hated the idea of integration, grew more violent, burning crosses and bombing homes of black families.

When the Ballet Russe headed into the South, Raven's family and friends worried. In some states, it was illegal for black dancers and white dancers to share the stage. Sometimes Raven lightened her skin with makeup.

Friends worried, but not Raven.
When Mr. Denham gave her the
solo waltz in *Les Sylphides*, she
filled the stage with joy and grace.

In 1957, their bus arrived in Atlanta, Georgia, and the dancers checked into a hotel. The hotel manager asked Raven if she was black, and Raven didn't lie. "I couldn't deny my very being and who I was," she said. The manager then ordered Raven to leave, afraid that the building might be bombed if she remained.

During the same tour, at a performance in Alabama, men rushed onstage shouting, "You all got a nigra in the company?" The dancers circled round and round, protecting Raven. "Nobody batted an eye, so the men had to go away," she said.

Later in the tour, Raven and her friends ate in their hotel dining room, watching parents and their children enjoy dinner. Then she noticed an empty chair piled high with white robes and hoods "like dirty old laundry. Parents were teaching children they loved to become instruments of hatred," said Raven.

That night, knowing it was risky, Raven chose not to perform. Instead, she stayed in her hotel and watched a cross burn from one of the windows. It could be seen for miles.

In one of the most famous ballets, *Swan Lake*, a single ballerina might perform as both a white swan and a black swan. Though Raven had danced solo roles, one of the company's ballet mistresses told Raven that a black dancer would never do *Swan Lake* in the Ballet Russe.

"They weren't going to have a black dancer portray a white swan," Raven said, "but I never understood why they couldn't have a black dancer be a black swan."

In 1962, after spending six years with the Ballet Russe, Raven knew it was time to go.

A devout Catholic who always felt drawn to the spiritual life, she joined a convent in 1963 to seek a clarity she was never able to achieve in performing.

A few years later in 1967, Raven was offered a position in the Dutch National Ballet in Holland. There, "people were far more interested in *who* I was rather than *what* I was," she said.

In Europe, as Madame Swoboda had once predicted, Raven danced before royalty: Queen Juliana of the Netherlands.

After seven years performing across Europe, Raven longed for home. In 1974, Raven returned to the United States. She joined the New York City Opera, dancing until 1985 (when she was fifty!) and taking on other acting roles until 2011, when the opera closed its doors for good.

In 2015, almost exactly sixty years after Raven joined the Ballet Russe, Misty Copeland became the first African American principal dancer with the American Ballet Theater. As both Odette and Odile in *Swan Lake*, she made front-page news, and the world applauded.

Misty credited Raven as being instrumental in helping her find her place in the ballet world. Raven was at the performance to celebrate.

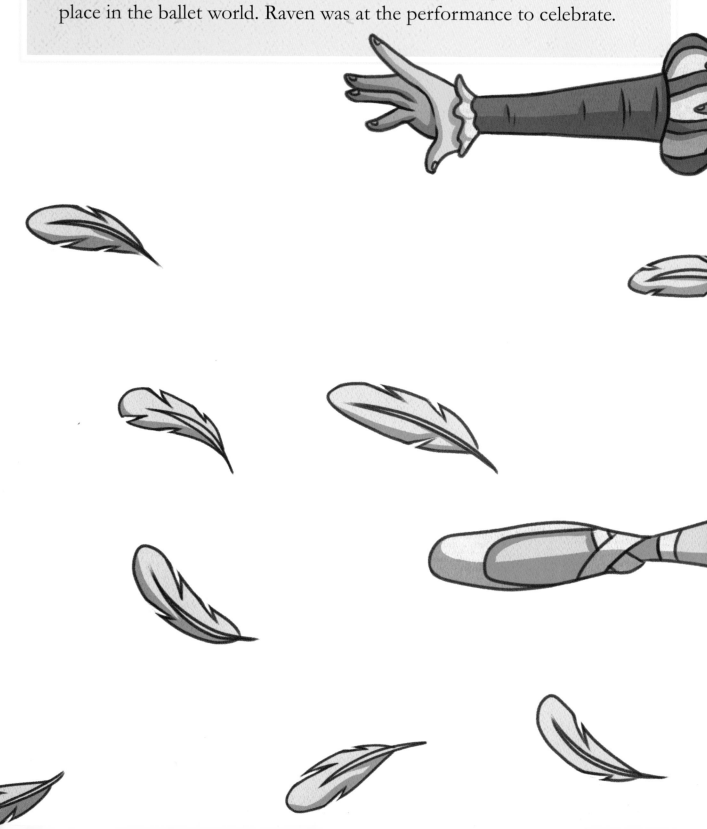

As the cheers rose like thunderclaps during the many curtain calls, Raven joined Misty onstage, and the two dancers joined hands. "She was a mentor in my life even before I met her," Misty said.

Raven Wilkinson, with her talent and courage, had led the way.

My Dear Young Friends,

Here is a book that I hope you will read and like. It is very special to me and I am so proud of it. I'll tell you why a little later.

It is the story of a little girl who loved to dance and wished with all her heart to become a ballet dancer. As she grew up and was trying very hard in her ballet classes, she realized that there were lots of obstacles in the way of her ever becoming a ballet dancer. But this is the story of her overcoming those obstacles by always following her dream and never giving up on the hope in her heart and the faith in herself.

As Mrs. Eleanor Roosevelt (the wife of President Franklin D. Roosevelt) once said, "The future belongs to those who believe in the beauty of their dreams."

Well, that little girl was me! And I am so proud and appreciative that our author, Leda Schubert, realized that this is a story about all of us and the hope that lights our way. It's a story that we all share.

With love,
Raven

ABOUT RAVEN WILKINSON

Ballet is incredibly difficult, requiring strength, grace, determination, and great talent. Raven faced an extra challenge: her skin color. As Raven said, "You're stretched to areas you think are impossible, and you see what you can achieve."

Anne Raven Wilkinson, known as Raven, was born on February 2, 1935, to Dr. Frost Bernie Wilkinson and Anne James Wilkinson. Her father went to Dartmouth and Harvard Medical School and became a dentist; her mother was a homemaker.

During her childhood, Raven lived with her parents and her brother, Frost, in the Dunbar apartment buildings in Harlem built by John D. Rockefeller, which were home to famous African Americans such as W. E. B. Du Bois, Paul Robeson, Asa Philip Randolph, Bill "Bojangles" Robinson, and Matthew Henson.

Raven attended the Ethical Culture Fieldston School in Riverdale, New York, before transfering to the Professional Children's School. Then she attended Columbia University, leaving to join the Ballet Russe, one of the major companies of the time.

The director, Sergei Denham, asked her parents if she wanted to "advertise" her color. Her parents replied that Raven would never misrepresent herself, and she did not. "I couldn't deny my very being and who I was. . . . Once you do it, you're stuck. You must always do it. You can't be seen with your family; you wonder what your children might look like. I wanted to be a total whole person," she said.

The only other African American dancer in a major company at the time was Janet Collins, who danced in New York with the Metropolitan Opera. Later, Lauren Anderson danced *Swan Lake* with the Houston Ballet.

Raven danced with the Ballet Russe from 1955 to 1962. The company disbanded in 1968. When she auditioned for other companies, people suggested she try African dance or jazz. "I was trained in ballet," Raven said. Raven spent seven months in a convent and then worked for a while but realized she wanted to dance again, and she did so for several more years in small ensembles. Then she went to Holland and remained with the Dutch National Ballet until she reached the forced retirement age of thirty-eight. Shortly thereafter, she came home and joined the New York City Opera, dancing and performing as a variety of characters.

According to those who saw her dance, Raven was a lyrical, romantic dancer, and she had a keen sense for acting roles.

When Raven was turned away from her first Ballet Russe audition, presumably because of the risks of traveling in the South, she said, "I am going to keep on knocking at that door even if some people would consider it battering your head against the wall. . . . I was going to keep on. So I did." In 2014, she remarked, "My never-ending question is: When are we going to get a Swan Queen of a darker hue?"

Only a year later, in 2015, her question was answered and she was able to say: "We feel ourselves in Misty going forward. Isn't that a wonderful thing?" That same year, Raven would receive the Dance/USA Trustees Award.

BALLET TERMS

Arabesque — \ˌa-rə-ˈbesk\: the dancer stands on one straight leg with an arm extended forward with the other arm and leg extended backward

Ballet mistress: a woman who directs, teaches, and rehearses dancers for a ballet company

Échappé — \¦ā͏ˌsha¦pā\: a level movement of both feet from a closed to an open position

Pirouette — \ˌpir-ə-ˈwet\: a complete turn of the body on one foot

Plié — \plē-ˈā\: a bending of the knee or knees

Second soloist: a dancer who has excelled in the ballet company and has been promoted to perform smaller group dances and some solo roles

PARTIAL BIBLIOGRAPHY

"[S]he was a mentor. . . ."
http://www.elle.com/culture/celebrities/news/a31168/misty-copeland-interview-a-ballerinas-tale.

"My never-ending question . . ."
http://pointemmagazine.com/inside-pt/issuesjunejuly-2014web-exclusive-interview-raven-wilkinson.

All other quotes: Schubert/interview with Raven Wilkinson.

Ballets Russes. Directed by Daniel Geller and Dayna Goldfine. New York City: Zeitgeist Films, 2006.

DanceUSA YouTube Channel. "Dance/USA 2015 Trustees Award Presentation." July 1, 2015.
https://www.youtube.com/watch?v=-kUolyXG-C0.

Deans, Joselli. "Black Ballerinas Dancing on the Edge: An Analysis of the Cultural Politics in Delores Browne's and Raven Wilkinson's Careers, 1954–1985." Ed.D. diss., Temple University, 2001.

Fuhrer, Margaret. "Web Exclusive—An Interview with Raven Wilkinson." *Pointe*, June 2, 2014.
www.pointemagazine.com/issues/junejuly-2014/web-exclusive-interview-raven-wilkinson.

Groskop, Viv. "Segregation Remains on the Stage." *New Statesman*, April 24, 2006.

Hampson, Sarah. "Raven Wilkinson: They Told Her a Black Person Couldn't Do Swan Lake."
Globe and Mail, December 17, 2005.

I'll Make Me a World. "The Dream Keepers." Directed by Sam Pollard. Produced by Blackside, Inc., in association with Thirteen/WNET New York. Virginia: PBS Video, 1999.

Kourlas, Gia. "Where Are All the Black Swans?" *New York Times*, May 6, 2007.

Langlois, Michael. "A Conversation with Raven Wilkinson," *Ballet Review*, Fall 2007, 22–32.

Schubert, Leda. Personal interview with Raven Wilkinson, April 12, 2009, New York City;
phone call with Raven Wilkinson, March 2, 2010.

Wisner, Heather. "Grace Under Fire—Dancer Raven Wilkinson." *Dance Magazine*, February 2001.

Zide-Booth, Rochelle. "Raven's Book." E-mail to Leda Schubert. February 12, 2010.